Walking Light

Christian Poetry

David LaChapelle

[28] And we know that in all things God works for the good of those who love him, who[i] have been called according to his purpose. [29] For those God foreknew he also predestined to be conformed to the image of his Son, that he might be the firstborn among many brothers and sisters. [30] And those he predestined, he also called; those he called, he also justified; those he justified, he also glorified.

Romans 8:28-30 (NIV)

ISBN: 9798375339627

POEMS

³ I thank my God every time I remember you. ⁴ In all my prayers for all of you, I always pray with joy ⁵ because of your partnership in the gospel from the first day until now, ⁶ being confident of this, that he who began a good work in you will carry it on to completion until the day of Christ Jesus.

Philippians 1:3-6 (NIV)

<u>Inspired</u>

Tonight, is the night

I am flowing like a river for words

They come to the page

I am delighted even more

I thought I would not,

Write another book,

For quite sometime

I guess you had other plans

You directed me to write these poems

Here I stand

To make another claim

Desire

I do not know what is in store

Am I out of here

Forevermore

Can you salvage my life

Do you have more

A plan to bring me higher than before

Or am I where I am supposed to be

And cannot see

The goodness all around

Only you can ever satisfy this hungry soul

Contentment

I just want to be content

I do not want to have to defend this tent

If I am all yours

Why do I suffer more?

If I am not all you made me to be

Take possession of my soul please

I invite you to lead me to the open door

I give you permission to take control

To be free

Hurry please

I cannot take these chains

And slay the giant

That has kept me enslaved

Your Way

Why are you so slow?

Why are you so deliberate?

So gentle and kind

Just take me by force Lord

Show me that you are mine

I want to understand the truth

About myself and know your way

So, I can rest and take it easy,

the rest of my days

<u>Needs</u>

I need to know

What you have in store

So, I can learn to trust

And have something to look forward too

And not always worry

That I will not have my way

But realize

You have me in the palm of your hands

That everything is going to be okay

And you have not forgotten,

about me and my future

Amazing grace

Leading

Speak to my heart

A drop of a tear to start

To open me up

To what you are about

To know you more

And what you have for me

That I am not alone

You will stand by my feet

Keeping me in step

Do not let me lead

Give me peace

So, I know I am doing the right thing

Harnessed

I speak of treasures of the heart

That I have ambition that won't quiet

I am like a crazy horse

That needs to be bridled and broken

I am so strong

You made me weak

To depend on you

And be in line with your direction

for life

To make me who I am meant to be

To harness my will to your heartbeat

Conflicted

I want everything Lord

I want nothing at all

I am conflicted

There is a war for my soul

The flesh against the spirit

Fighting for control

You will not let me have my way

Blessings are around the corner

I do not have to wait anymore

Thank you, Lord,

Human

I feel guilty

I feel ashamed

That I am so human

I am so inadequate

So vulnerable

So dependent

That I want more out of life

I cannot take hurt and strife

I see pain all around

I am helpless to lend a hand

You make me limited

I guess that is my testimony

Be lifted

Quiet Time

All alone in this room

The night takes its colors in bloom

Quietness is everywhere

Just the sound over my shoulders

You will take me where I need to go

You will equip me

For the task at hand

Help me be

The best man I can

I am all yours

Show me the greater plan

<u>Being</u>

You will not take me by force

You will not shove your will

Down my throat

I want more than to be led by you

I want to participate

In being in control

Knowing I have made lasting contributions

Help me to see

The good you have for me

Today

Adventure

You are the reason

I believe

In something more

Then what I see

It is an ambition

My soul craves

A thirst nobody can satisfy

But only your grace

That is why I strive to you

All these years

Never giving up hope

But knowing you are by my side

Along for the ride

<u>Rescued</u>

I am at the edge

There is nowhere to go

There is no backing out

I have dumped my baggage

I am in a room

I am ready to fall

You will catch me when

I am small

To the promised land

To the unknown forest

You will show me where to go

You will show me an open door

I just keep the course

Do not look back

Let go

I am getting lighter

The structures around my mind

Has evaded

Done chasing feelings

I have been found out

I am glad

Passage

I need you Lord

To walk anew

Light on the foot

I am letting go

Trading cautious for living

Consequences are a part of life

If you do not take a chance

You will not see

The fulfilment of destiny

If I fall

You will pick me up

Moving forward

Is what it is all about

To see the setting of the sun

Clothed in fine linen

To part the clouds for love

Facing the unknown

Embracing belief's place

Testing the testimony of faith

Illuminating my path with your Word

Has come to pass

Locked In

I was made for you

I feel that now

I belong in your arms

Your holy presence is mine

I have faltered

What was there is gone

There is no reason to cope

with the past anymore

Those lonely nights were not in vain

You spoke to my heart

I got to understand how you think

I am connected

I cannot stray

Even if I sin

You always take me back

You have me locked in your grace

<u>Over Myself</u>

I feel whole and complete

The struggle is over to compete

Peace is here

I am open to being me now

Transparency and reality are pure

Nothing to wrestle with

Just shed a quiet tear

For all those lost years

Meant something to me

More than words can describe

You are taking me somewhere new

Where you will need me too

And all I have is belief

And a testimony to see

You are up to something good

Whatever you have planned

I will be your man

No one can stop you

What you are about to do

The time is ripe

The fruit is ready to pick

I can feel your grace upon me

I can feel your power around

Miracles are about to be performed

I am at the open door

I am reformed

Transformed

I am loved

I can see the pain was not you

There is a load off my back

A forgotten identity no longer resides

Within this human form

You are not disappointed

Your work

Is evident for all to see

You changed me from the inside out

To get up and walk

To an open door

Where I belong

Back home

United and whole

When I wake up

Why?

You are all to me

I belong to you

You have set me aside

For this special time

Because you know me inside out

There is no other way

But to go to your throne

Where you will welcome

Me with open arms

And then I will know what this

Is all for

Life is so much more

Guidance

I need your touch Lord

In my life and about

Your ways are steady and sure

Gentle and refined

I prayed for favor

In your own timing

It has come forth

I have been at the bottom

Just cutting wood

I have been there for sometime

Had to come to the end

Of what I was programmed to follow

It is quiet and comforting

To see your handiwork come to pass

Since I first believed in your glorious name

The Fold

The heavens shake

The earth quakes

The clouds part

Sun shining through the skies

It is all you

Coming full of glory

And the love we all crave

All these days

Humanity has been through

Then we will know

What all this life was meant for

Striving to send the good

Has come back to you

Your return is never on hold

We are told to wait for more

Substance

I do not have the strength to read

I do not have the faith to believe

I do not have the interest in your Word

I need to reconnect with you

Pull me through

Please hear my plea

I will just talk and tell you how I feel

Until I come to the point

That I know you are real

Returning

Forgive me Lord

For my rebellion

My running away from you

In another direction

I could not get too far from your love

You were not surprised by my move

You knew what I would do

Before time began

You know me inside and out

I feel so loved

That you have not let me go on my own

You brought me back

You restored my faith

It is all because of you

Struggle

You brought me back into the fold

I did not believe until you showed me

Your love

I tried to run; I tried to hide

I was fooling myself

It was my pride

I did know what else to do

I could not cope with what you

Put me through

I told you I had enough

I came to the end

I fell off the edge of the cliff

You caught in mid air

Here I am

A new beginning

<u>Waiting</u>

I believe in you Lord

For whatever this is for

It is beyond my scope of expertise

You keep teaching me

Patience please

Your divine plan

Cannot be interrupted

It is not my responsibility

I just must play my part

And you will be with me

To be vulnerable and secure

Into the grace of your loving arms

Life

Forgive me Lord

For trying to run away from you

Help me trust you Lord

That you know what to do

I went on a walk

Came full circle

Now I am looking at you

To be my rescue

To save me from myself

To bring me to the end

To empty me out

And give me a new beginning

I want to see victory in this life

Do not make all my labor for the afterlife

Stepping Out

I want to know you

I want to feel your touch

I want to see your handiwork

Manifest in my life

I do not want to see this as a coincidence

But your master plan in action

Being the evidence

So, I have something to hold onto

And make an altar

To have a reason to worship you

Other than being a soldier in the battlefield

<u>All</u>

Forgive me Lord

For what I am trying to prove

I need you Jesus

More than the cares of this life

We need to get reacquainted

I will tell you how I feel

I know you will hear me

Because you want me

To know you are real

You always take me back

I do not have to be ashamed

It is part of being human

It is just who you made me to be

You have a plan

I cannot stray too far off course

Your love gently calling me forth

Where it is safe and harmony is found

Where I am not alone

This is where I belong

In the loving arms of Jesus

The one who created it all

Promises

Do not leave me Lord

Please show me what to do

Help me depend on you

So, I can be true

And do what is right

And love while it is still day

To be the man

You want me to be

No matter where I will be found

I will not make a sound

Just trusting quietly in you

That your promises will come through

Love Me

Oh Lord

Please do not loosen your grip on me

Hold me tightly

So, I can breathe

I need you Jesus for life itself

That is where meaning is to be found

In the comfort of your hands

Working all through my forgotten plans

Let me know

I am not doing this all by myself

I need to know you care Lord

And have me all to yourself

Eternity

The enemy fought tooth and nail

But he did not prevail

I came to the end

Without fighting the graves

Resurrected and secure

His plan is for sure

I am on the waiting list

For His graceful wish

To spend eternity

Where we belong

And will not hide my face

But know my place

Forevermore

Realization

Rise up

Rise up

The time is ripe

To make our calling complete

A sure steady feat

To an opening

We have been longing for

On this narrow path of hope

To breathe and catch our breath

To get a glimpse of His breadth

And realize why we were made

For Victory

Creation

The time has come

For the setting of the sun

When things will be made clear

There is nothing to fear

This is what we have been created for

To walk through the open door

Where we will know

Who we are

Made in His image

The likeness is a resemblance

In harmony and paradise

A mirror of His grace

We will be one day

Immersed in His loving ways

Progress

A new tune to sing

A life full of strings

Conduct me Lord

That sounds different than before

A way to dance the night for more

I am ready to pull through

Instead of going through the motions

To flow with commotion

And live the way

I am meant to be

What makes me happy

My own responsibility

For good or bad

I will make my way to you

Newness

You have my heart

Dismantling my defences

Emptying me out

Of what I thought I was about

To be a vessel of your love

The world needs

Including me

Help me to understand Lord

You are making things new

So, I just look to you

And be aware,

You have me locked in your grace

Forevermore

Transparency

Keep me pure

My thoughts my reservoir

Empty me out

So, I can open up

And share how you think

In me

Not the world's affairs

Or operation of the times

Walk a fine line

Paved with gold

That cannot be moved

Distinct

Fair for all who want the real deal

The End

Courage not needed here

There is nowhere to go

There is nothing else to do

You will have all of me soon

Your love shining through

I give up my ways

I am at the end of trying to believe

That means there is a new beginning

When you will take me

I do not know

If you make me a testimony

Or do you have a life for me here

Is there more work to do

Or when you make me whole

Take me home

Lead me

You know what to do

You are in complete control

I am at the end of my rope

You know my ways when you come for me

And glory to your grace

ABOUT THE AUTHOR

David LaChapelle is a born-again Christian living with Paranoid Schizophrenia since the year 2000. David has earned himself two Computer Technical Diplomas from Seneca College in Toronto, Canada in 1994 and 1996. He graduated with a Psychology degree in 2011 from Trent University in Peterborough, Canada where he now calls home. David lives a quiet life and enjoys writing and being an author. He is proud of his works and hopes it will bring him recognition in this life and rewards hereafter. David is a firm believer in reading the Word of God and the power of prayer and wishes the best for all humanity waiting for the Lord's return.

OTHER BOOKS BY DAVID LACHAPELLE

David's Adventure with Schizophrenia: My Road to Recovery

David's Journey with Schizophrenia: Insight into Recovery

David's Victory Thru Schizophrenia: Healing Awareness

David's Poems: A Poetry Collection

1000 Canadian Expressions and Meanings: EH!

Freedom in Jesus

Canadian Slang Sayings and Meanings: Eh!

The Biggest Collection of Canadian Slang: Eh!

Healing Hidden Emotions for Believers

Breaking Clouds: Christian Poetry

All books and e-books available at Amazon

Manufactured by Amazon.ca
Bolton, ON